The
Enikma Philosophy

An intentional career,
a purposeful life

Katherine Woollard

First published in 2024 by EKP Books

ISBN (print): 978-1-7384283-0-4
ISBN (ebook): 978-1-7384283-1-1

To Stu, Jay, Ryan and Philippa

– my tribe.

Contents

About the author

Katherine Woollard is an experienced senior leader in digital, innovation and marketing. She has worked across multiple organisations and industries from Financial Services to Non-Profit.

She is passionate about people development and a firm believer that everyone has the capacity to grow and develop themselves. Through her work she has been motivated to write this book to provide the tools and inspiration which will help people to make intentional choices in their work-life. Enabling them to have the life that is purposeful and important for them as individuals.

She has been an active mentor and coach for many years and in lots of different capacities. What matters to her most is seeing others not just survive work but thrive in their work lives. Whatever that might look like.

She is also a wife, mother of three, avid crafter and does lots of other irrelevant things for this author bio. But they're important to her, so worth a mention.

She would love to hear from you if you've enjoyed this book or not. As someone with a passionate belief in self-development, she is always open to learning more and evolving her thoughts and practice based on new knowledge. So, please do get in touch with your thoughts or stories.

Email: katherine.woollard@enikma.co.uk

LinkedIn: katherinewoollard

The
Enikma Philosophy

An intentional career,
a purposeful life

The

Introduction

The Enikma philosophy is based on the learnings from a variety of different ideas across both modern and ancient times. From the Stoicism philosophy of the Ancient Greeks, to Minimalism born in the art culture of the 60s and 70s, to the most recent Slow Living movement. We'll look at all of these as we move through the book along with other schools of thought. They all have slightly different takes on things, and some seem more relevant today than others. But through them all is a golden thread of trying to make life better, more intentional and more purposeful.

These philosophies are much broader than just career, and many of them don't really touch on it at all. But there are significant learnings which have fed into the creation of the three pillars of the Enikma Philosophy for developing an intentional career.

A good place to start is asking why it focuses on career and work-life. Throughout time, work has made up a significant part of our lives, both in terms of time and where we spend our energy. Trying to improve your overall life and wellbeing without considering your work-life is just tinkering around the edges. The approach presented here can be applied to almost any area of your life, but I'm focusing on work because in my experience it is often the one place that is most at odds with the life we'd like to be living.

So, what is the Enikma Philosophy and why should you care about it?

Ultimately, it is intended to be a simple set of guiding principles which are easy to remember, easy to apply and have a profound impact on your wellbeing, enjoyment of your life and the value you bring. I strongly believe that keeping it simple is good for everything and with that in mind, you'll find this book is intentionally written in simple language and is kept short to respect your time. It can be easy to be drawn into spending a lot of time reading and thinking about being intentional and purposeful, rather than actually doing it. I have no desire for this book to add to that.

You should be able to start implementing the ideas in this book straight away. It's not complicated and it doesn't exclude anyone based on their experiences, education or personal circumstances. The approach is just as applicable to you whether you are a senior executive working at a desk all day, or a barista making people's days just that bit better with a coffee and a smile.

The Enikma Philosophy is all about you. What's important to you as an individual, and how you are going to make your work-life work better for you. Our society is built to constantly tell us what should matter to us, but this is dictated by other people's agendas and marketers trying to sell you things or make you behave in certain ways. And I say this as a professional marketer – I promise we're generally good people!

That's enough about why I've developed this philosophy. So, now it's time to share it...

There are three simple pillars:

1. Know what matters

2. Do only what matters

3. Do more of what matters

Bit of an anti-climax?

Well, I did say it was simple by design. Even if all you take from this book is those three things and apply them in your own way, that would likely have results for you. But the rest of this book will explore ways to use this framework to think differently, work differently, and build a work-life which is authentic to you, intentionally chosen and gives you meaning and purpose.

Part 1

Know what matters

Know what matters

This first part focuses on making sure you are clear on what is important to you. It will look at how you set your direction and how you develop clarity about what you want your work-life to provide for you and how it will fit into your wider life.

There are two key elements to this - Values and Purpose.

Values define how you want to work, and how you want others to work with and treat you. If values are the 'how', then purpose is the 'what'. What do you want to achieve? What will give you job satisfaction and mean that your work-life is a positive element of your overall life?

The following two chapters will explore values and purpose in more detail. They suggest some activities you might want to try which explore your own values and purpose. You can approach them in either order. It's important to understand both when making career decisions, but you may find one or the other a better place to start. Sometimes either values or purpose is really clear to us whilst the other is much harder to get to the bottom of.

Whilst values and purpose can be approached in either order, you need to have clarity around them both before you can move onto part two, 'Do only what matters'. It's impossible to focus only on what matters if you don't know what matters to you.

It might seem simple and straightforward and that everyone should know what matters to them. But, in my experience, breaking through the noise of what society tells us should matter to us day in and day out, to get to the real truth inside us, can take longer and be more difficult than we might imagine. There are lots of psychological reasons why this is, and we'll touch on them lightly throughout. But, this book is action-oriented. If you're interested in deeper learnings around how our brains work, there's loads of information and studies out there which you will likely find fascinating. However, be aware of the trap of avoiding doing the difficult work of actually making change by spending far too long reading about it.

1 - Values

Our values are what make us who we are as individuals. They drive our decisions, the people we choose to spend time with, our political views and the causes we are passionate about. They are the deep-held views we hold about ourselves and the world around us.

Our values do change and evolve over time, they are developed through our experiences. As we learn and experience more, our values will flex and develop with us. We are also shaped by those around us, both those we know well and those who influence us in our wider society. Our values reflect what we fundamentally believe is right and wrong, and how that manifests through our beliefs, behaviours and actions.

So, how do we know what our values are?

In my experience, we usually only have a small number of core values. I believe three is a good number to aim for identifying. We aren't one dimensional so one is unlikely to paint a true picture of us, but more than three reduces the focus on what really matters. Working out which yours are can be, and almost always is, harder than we expect and needs some deep reflection and thinking. But, the process itself is simple.

Often, it's easier to recognise when things don't fit your values than when they do. We can have both a physical and emotional reaction to things which don't align to our values. Whether it's an underlying uncomfortable feeling in your gut or outright anger and outrage. Finding your values is about focusing on those feelings to find what doesn't work for you. You'll then start to recognise what sits well with you and feels comfortable and authentic.

There are a few activities you can use to work out what your values are. They are outlined in the activity boxes on the following pages. You might want to use one of these or try all three.

If you want any of these exercises to be helpful, you need to be absolutely honest with yourself. There are no rights and wrongs here. Your values can be absolutely anything and you are the only person who needs to know what they are. Your values are who you are, whether you admit it to yourself or not. By trying to be someone else or choosing things you think are 'better' than you, all you are doing is assuming someone else's values are more important or correct than yours. They aren't. All values are created equal. The things that are most important to you are just that. You can't make the things that are important to you important to someone else, but they can't change yours either. You are the only person who can really know what your values are, and you are the only person with the power to evolve them, if you want to, over time.

So, with that in mind, why not try one or more of the following activities to understand what your core values really are. These activities look at your values from three different perspectives:

1. How you see others

2. How you're seen by others

3. How you see yourself

Activity 1 – How you see others

Sometimes it can be hard to look at ourselves directly, especially if we're lacking confidence or feeling a bit lost. So, it can be helpful to look outside of ourselves to start with. Using others as a mirror to our own values.

Think about some people you admire. Not the ones you want to be with, but those people you wish you could be more like. It might be people in the public eye, friends or family members, or people you work with or for. Anyone you look up to for any reason. Write down the words you would use to describe them. You might want to do this for 5-10 different people.

Take a look at the words.

Have you used the same words for a number of the people?

Have you got words which link together – for example, honest, transparent, trustworthy?

Maybe highlight the ones which feel most important in why you admire them.

If you see themes in the words you've chosen, try to narrow them down to one of the words in the group.

Keep grouping and narrowing until you have 3 words.

Say each word on your list.

How do you feel? Do they sit comfortably with you? If not, go back to your list and see if one of the others feels more 'right' to you.

Say 'I am...(each word)'.

Does this feel comfortable to you? If not, think about whether you want it to be who you are or you feel you 'ought' to want it to be. Make sure all the words are things you are able to or want to be able to say comfortably about yourself.

Activity 2 – How you're seen by others

As with the first exercise, this activity uses our desire to be validated by others to help us understand ourselves. And to be clear, this is a normal human need for belonging. Needing external validation is what drives social media and whilst it can have its downsides, these come from people exploiting the need, rather than the need itself. So, if this is more comfortable for you than looking directly inward that's absolutely fine.

For this exercise ask yourself:

If other people I know were asked to describe me in three words, which three words would I like them to use?

It is really important to think about which words you would 'like' them to use rather than what they might actually use. We are sometimes forced to behave in ways which don't align to our values, and we also often have a skewed understanding of how others view us. By focusing on our wishes, these impacts can be removed.

Which words come to mind, jot them down.

You can come up with more than three at this point. Just note down all the words you'd want to be described with.

As with the last exercise, take a look at them. Are there themes in the words? Can you group them together and narrow them down by choosing the one out of a group which feels better for you?

Keep grouping and narrowing until you have 3 which feel right to you.

Say 'People describe me as...' followed by your words. Note how you feel. Does it feel like you? Do any of the words feel uncomfortable at all? If so, look back at your list. Does another one feel more you?

Once you've completed this exercise and if you want to, you can actually ask people the question and see what they say. Do you see any patterns? Do your family, friends and work colleagues see you the same way, and the same way you see yourself or would like to see yourself?

Activity 3 – How you see yourself

The final way to approach this exercise is to look at a pre-written list of values and choose the ones which resonate most with you. There are lots of different lists of values to start from. I'd suggest a quick search on the web and choose one. You can always add your own if they don't have quite the word you need.

Go through the list fairly quickly with a highlighter or ticking the ones that resonate with you.

As with the previous exercises, the next step is to start grouping and narrowing your choices. Group together into themes and choose the word that sits most comfortably with you from each or add a new one if the one you're looking for isn't there. Then keep doing the same thing until you've whittled it down to 3.

Say to yourself 'My values are... (your 3 words)'.

How does that feel. Do you feel a sense of peace with the words, do they make you want to smile? If not, revisit your choices.

Another good check is to look at the ones you've discarded and see how you feel about them not being in your list. If you feel really uncomfortable with them missing, they are likely to be a core value for you.

If you've done more than one of these exercises you might find you still have more than three words. Keep grouping and narrowing until you have the three which feel most right to you.

This list of three words is what you've identified as your values. I strongly recommend sitting with them for a couple of weeks. Why not jot them on a post-it note and stick them to your screen or in your notebook, or put them on the home screen of your phone. How do you feel every time you see them?

Trust your gut here. If they don't feel quite right, take the time to go back to your lists and see if there's something else which feels more authentically you.

Time spent really making sure these are right for you is time well spent. You'll be using these values to help you make choices about what you do in the future, so if they aren't really true to you, you could end up making decisions which aren't right for you as a result.

One of my clients summed up the feeling of comfort beautifully in a group session. She said she felt everyone else would choose better values and hers seemed really basic and obvious. Of course, everyone else felt theirs were really obvious too, but no two people had chosen the same words. And, actually that's a sign of you having picked the right things. It should feel obvious to you. They are your core values. This isn't the time to overthink, it's the time to rely on your intuition, feelings and emotions. The more you think, the more you will let other people's opinions in. This is about you and only you. No one else, not even your nearest loved ones can tell you what your values are. They can tell you how they see you, but only you know whether that aligns with who you really are deep down.

Take time, be honest and be true to you.

The impact of your values on your relationships

Once you're really comfortable with your values, you'll start to see the impact they have on the people and relationships you have around you. The things that matter most to you are the things that you'll value most in other people.

Obviously, this raises a question... if we all have different values, surely, we won't ever get what we need from other people?

This isn't the case at all. As you saw from your initial lists, lots of values are likely to be important to you. Your core values are the ones which are the MOST important.

For example, imagine one of your core values is honesty. This means honesty is non-negotiable for you. Most people would say honesty is important and try to be honest as much as possible. However, when someone is dishonest with you it is likely to be a deal-breaker. You are very unlikely to be able to forgive and forget because it goes against something that is so deeply rooted in your belief system. For others, they may think honesty is a good thing, but for them other values are more important so find it easier to move past it when someone is dishonest with them. It's these kinds of things where people can find the reactions of others completely incomprehensible. What can seem like a massive overreaction to one person, is likely to be due to one of their core values being challenged. The more we can understand each other's core values, the more we can build effective relationships.

The impact of your values on your career choices

Sometimes, getting clarity on your values can be like a 'light-bulb moment' in understanding challenges or high points you have experienced in your career. You may have worked for an organisation which had values that completely aligned with yours and felt in tune with you. Or you might have experienced organisational values that jarred against your core values and made working there incredibly difficult. Sometimes it can be your manager, rather than the entire organisation which drives this feeling.

Either way, having a value fit with the organisation is vital to job satisfaction. Anything which forces us to act in a way which goes against our core values on an ongoing basis is going to have serious impacts on our wellbeing, mental health and even physical health. That's why choosing your employer carefully is really important.

It doesn't matter what kind of work you are doing, there will be a culture and an expectation around behaviours. This is going to be made up for a mixture of the history of the organisation, the leadership (at every level) and the reward systems in place. When considering where you want to work, it's important to look at all three.

Starting with the history of the organisation. Cultural evolution and change takes time and a conscious effort. It's much easier to keep doing the same things you've always done. And, if the same people are asked to do the same things and achieve the same results, they will continue to do it in the same ways unless something significantly changes. Just changing the stated values or culture of an organisation won't change anything unless the systems, structures and practices of the past are also changed to reflect the new values.

You often see this in practice when organisations make a strategy change. It is usually followed by a restructure to realign the organisation to the new direction. There are often redundancies both voluntary and not. Effectively this is the organisation choosing what they now value and some people making the decision it doesn't fit with them anymore (although there are often other reasons people choose to take voluntary redundancy). This is fairly functional, but what happens in the following year to 18 months is where values really start to come into play. In my experience, there is always a second wave of leavers following a restructure. These are the people who keep a job during the restructure, but don't fit the organisation culturally anymore. Quite often it's the people who were seen as high-performers in the previous culture who are suddenly no longer seen that way, but as blockers or disruptive. They are likely to be resistant to the change and to be central to any discontent, trying to build a resistance movement with their colleagues. In the majority of cases they will leave within a short period of time either by their choice or the organisation's.

So, the history can tell you a lot about what is valued and why you might see pockets of discontent especially after a significant change.

The leadership of an organisation is also a key indicator of the values. When an organisation has stated values, they are likely to closely reflect or match the values of the owner or chief executive. And if they don't, expect a refresh. Our values are the things that are obvious to us and just make sense, so it's really unlikely that the person giving final sign off of the values of an organisation doesn't think the most important ones to reflect are the most important ones to them personally. The words might be slightly different, but the sentiments will align.

The stated values are just one element though. Throughout the organisation, subcultures will develop within departments and teams based on the leadership of those areas. Most of the time these won't be hugely dissimilar to the overall culture, but sometimes you can see drastic differences. It's likely that the most influential person in shaping the culture of your team will be your line manager, so when thinking about a job, ask them questions about what's important to them and it will tell you a lot about whether you have a good values fit.

It's important to remember that sharing similar values doesn't mean you lack diversity of thought. This is about how you go about what you do, not that you have to agree on everything.

The final element which shapes workplace culture and values is the reward systems in place. This is not necessarily the stated rewards, but what is recognised and what is ignored in how objectives are reached. For example, if you are working in an organisation with a clear sales target, you can tell a lot about the organisation by how people work to achieve it. If no action is taken against people who knowingly over promise to make a sale and they get the rewards and recognition for their sales figures as a result, you are unlikely to fit if honesty or integrity are your key values. However, if drive or ambition are key to you, you might be completely comfortable with this and thrive in this type of environment. Remember, neither is right or wrong. Your core values don't mean you don't think that other values are also good, they just aren't your absolute top priorities and not having them is unlikely to impact your wellbeing or health.

It's important to take all of these things into account when thinking about your career moves and the questions you would ask a prospective employer. Recruitment processes are definitely a two-way process. You need to be sure you want to work for them as much as they need to be sure they want you.

As someone who has interviewed a lot of prospective employees, I find it really surprising how few have questions for me prepared. Not only is it widely recognised as good interview practice, it is the candidate's opportunity to explore what matters to them about the role or the organisation. It's also the bit the interviewer hasn't prepared for, so you get to see them in a much more normal and natural way.

But before you get to the point of interviewing for other roles, it's worth understanding your fit where you currently are.

Activity 4 – Your values alignment

Think about your current work. How well does it align to your values? Ask yourself the following questions:

What are the stated values of the organisation (if they have any), how do they make you feel?

Do you see an alignment between how your owner/Chief Executive behave and communicate and the stated values?

What do you think the values are that you see from the leaders in your direct line?

Are people rewarded in line with the stated values?

Based on the answers to these questions, how well do you feel you are aligned to the organisation you currently work for? Does anything contradict your core values?

If you are struggling at work or dealing with workplace stress, you might find that the activity above gives you some clarity about why. Likewise, if you see a good level of alignment, it may help you understand why you feel job satisfaction and are happy at the organisation. Either way, knowing what matters to you in terms of values can really help you when you are at a point when you need to make decisions about your career.

Managing a values mis-alignment

If, through the last activity, you have realised you have a values mis-match with your organisation, your manager or the leadership in your department, you will need to think about how you manage this. You have a few options:

1. Find another role in another organisation

2. Find another role in another department or team

3. Make changes to the things you can control to move to a more aligned position in your current role

The first is relatively simple. If you know your organisation and really don't feel it's a good fit for you and there's nothing you could change to make it better, it's probably time to move on. If there is no ambition within the organisation to change (and there likely won't be unless there's been a recent change in senior leadership) then focus your attentions on finding something where you can comfortably be yourself. And make sure you use the interview process to really check alignment with the new organisation.

Sometimes you might be aligned to the stated values of the organisation and see other teams which have subcultures which match your values much more, but you don't have that in your current team. You will know the cause of this intuitively. If it's that your line or department manager doesn't align to the values of the organisation, consider whether that is likely to change in terms of their behaviours. If they are a new employee, their behaviours will take time to adjust from the culture of their previous organisation. If they are a more long-term employee and have resolutely continued to behave in a way that doesn't align to the values of the organisation, and you, look for opportunities to move internally.

If you think you have the opportunity to change things to help with that alignment, then it can be worth working with your manager to see what changes you could make together. Sometimes managers just aren't aware until someone provides feedback, and sometimes they need the support of people in their team to help make change happen in the circles where they can influence.

2 - Purpose

So, our values tell us how we want to be and how we want to be treated. But purpose is much more about what we want to be doing and achieving.

It's important to start by saying that purpose isn't equally important at work for everyone. Some people are very purpose-driven and others just aren't. And wherever you sit on that spectrum is absolutely fine. It's also important to be clear that purpose isn't all about doing good for others, working for a charitable organisation or having to settle for less prestigious or materially rewarding roles. Purpose can be anything, including improving your skills in what you do, whatever that is.

Whether you are driven by a bigger purpose or not, having a goal to work towards can be the difference between having meaning in what you do and not. There is evidence which shows that having meaning in your life leads to higher levels of happiness, so it makes sense that having meaning in your career will help to generate job satisfaction.

It all starts with working out what really matters to you. Once you know that, you can understand the role your career plays in doing that. Your career (or the outcomes of your work) may be the thing that matters most, or it may be an enabler for the things outside of work which matter more to you. There is no obligation for what you do at work to be the most important thing, and for most of us it probably isn't. However, once we do understand the role of our jobs in our purpose, we then need to work out how to develop work which actively supports that. It will also help us to be able to be more productive and able to prioritise using the same thinking processes.

What does success mean to you?

Success is a difficult concept. At its most basic level it's achieving our goals. And it's this basic level that we will be getting to. As with most of this book, keeping it simple and being true to yourself is going to be key.

But, in terms of understanding your own definition of success, it's important to understand the impact living in a capitalist, always-on society has on us. Our society continually tells us we need more. More money, more stuff, more status, more followers, more likes, and on... and on... But, do any of these really mean we're successful or is it just that by making us constantly want more we continue to consume and keep the money machine moving?

If these things really did make us happy, which let's face it is most people's ultimate goal, then the richest, most popular people would be the happiest. It doesn't take long to realise that all the evidence tells us that money, status and fame can do the very opposite. Yet many people continue to chase after them relentlessly, even if they don't align to their values or purpose.

How often have you felt that your successes at work, no matter what they are, are an anti-climax because you've already moved your thinking on to what's next?

The money myth

We are inundated constantly with messages telling us that if we just have the latest thing, more money or enough likes on Instagram we'll be happy. We work hard doing things we don't really like to buy stuff which promises happiness, but what we get is the same life but with another thing in it. The dopamine hit of buying the thing gives us an illusion of happiness, but like any drug, it doesn't actually change anything other than the money in your bank account.

Don't get me wrong, some things can be really important for enabling a better life. Whether it's a car which enables you to get places more quickly and frees up your time, or a home of your own which gives you security and safety. But the improvements to our lives aren't the things themselves, they are what the things enable.

So, more money in and of itself won't bring us a happier life, but it can enable you to have access to more experiences which do enrich your life. Understanding the difference between what you are aiming towards and what the enablers are can help to change your mindset and break the belief that money or things bring happiness.

Happiness or contentedness

One of the other things to be aware of is that happiness is a transient thing. It's a peak of emotion. It's unrealistic to maintain a peak of emotion for an extended period. Much of the messaging around self-improvement is focused on achieving a state of permanent happiness. This continues to feed the same mechanisms that tell us we are never enough and need more to be successful.

It can be more helpful to think about reaching a sustained position of contentedness where we are comfortable with what we have and who we are. This is a completely realistic goal. Contentedness is the absence of negative elements such as stress, frustration or anger. It is a really powerful place to be, and often means you are more open to opportunities and taking measured risks.

Setting your purpose or goal

It's important to understand the difference between purpose and goals. Goals help us to achieve our purpose, but without purpose, goals can be achieved without being truly meaningful for us.

So, let's start with purpose.

Your purpose is the thing that drives you, and like your values, it's completely and wonderfully unique to you. There are different ways to think about what your purpose is and, don't worry, it will most likely change throughout different periods of your life.

Again, there are a couple of different exercises you might want to try to determine what your purpose is. You could try one of these or all of them, some might feel more comfortable than others to you.

Activity 1 – Looking back

I'm sure we've all heard people saying that 'when we're on our deathbed we aren't going to care about work' but what are we going to care about?

This is about imagining yourself in that very position. Think forward to the end of your healthy and successful life, you've put into practice all your learnings and have focused where it really matters. You're lying there listening to people around your bedside talking about your achievements and the things they remember most about you.

Close your eyes and listen. What are they saying?

What would you like them to say about you and the impact you had?

It could be what an amazing parent, grandparent or friend you were. It could be that you fought for social justice and changed people's lives. It could be that you always had the most amazing stories of your travels and adventures.

As you listen to these in your mind. Consider how they make you feel. If they only said one thing, what would you like it to be?

Activity 2 – Your life award

It may feel more comfortable to think forward rather than backwards. Close your eyes and imagine you are preparing for an awards ceremony. You know you're getting an award but you don't know what for.

What is the award you'd most like to win?

Design the award title. It could literally be anything. This is your award for being the best you that you can be.

What would success look like to you?

Who is giving you the award?

Announce your award to yourself. How does that feel? Which one gives you a true sense of satisfaction and pride?

Activity 3 – Your Wikipedia page

If public recognition and awards aren't your thing, think about what you'd like people to put on your Wikipedia page. It's all facts and evidence and the community make sure it remains good quality so you don't need to think about how it might be 'fluffy'. So, what would you want them to mention in your page about who you are and what your impact has been.

Are there any key facts or stats you'd want to be used to measure your impact?

All of these are about trying to think about what you'd like to be famous for. It's often the easiest way to understand how we'd like to see ourselves, to reflect what we'd like others to see and say about us. We are social animals, so that recognition and belonging is important to us. It also means that we often use the validation of others and we're wired to do so.

You can only have one purpose. There are likely to be lots of facets to who you are which you'd like to be recognised for, but you need to find the one which matters more than any other to you right now. And the one you can impact by doing things now. Remember, purpose is flexible over time. What matters to you most today won't necessarily be in the same in 5-10 years. Ask almost any new parent and they will likely be prioritising being a great parent, but that probably wasn't their no. 1 purpose 5 years earlier nor will it be 20 years later. Not because they don't want to be a great parent throughout life, but the amount of focus it has in their lives' changes.

We are an amalgamation of all the purposes we have focused on throughout our lives.

But, knowing which is our number 1 focus today is what we need. It means we can then focus on it and really ensure that we aren't distracted by using our time, attention and effort on things that aren't that important to us or are actually someone else's priority not our own.

Your purpose may or may not be linked to your work-life. Either is fine and the next chapters will look at how you can use your work-life to support your purpose, whichever domain your purpose sits in.

Your purpose statement

Now you've identified your purpose it's time to turn it into something really clear, unambiguous and helpful to you. Ideally, one sentence which sums it up as concisely as possible and feels completely comfortable to you.

You might want to start with jotting down words that come to mind when you are thinking about your purpose. They may be some of the words you imagined people using about you in the exercises above.

Now try to create a sentence starting with 'My purpose is to...'.

It can be tempting to overcomplicate it. But the simpler it is, the easier it is for you to remember and get behind. Some examples might be...

- *My purpose is to travel to all the places on my bucket list with my partner.*

- *My purpose is to raise as much money as I can for cancer charities in remembrance of my sister.*

- *My purpose is to spend as much time in nature as possible.*

- *My purpose is to be the best Grandparent I can be.*

Remember, this is your vision for you. You only need to worry about how you feel about it. You don't need to share it with anyone if you don't want to. If it seems basic and obvious it's probably about right. What's obvious to you won't be obvious to someone else because it won't align to the things that matter to them.

Like with your values, it's worth taking some time to sit with your purpose. Say it to yourself every morning for a couple of weeks. How does it feel? Really think about your physical and emotional reaction to it. It should feel empowering, inspiring and completely natural. If you haven't been totally honest with yourself, it just won't quite feel right.

We are all facing constant social pressures to be a certain way and value certain things, so actually being totally honest with ourselves about what we want, not what's expected of us can be a real challenge. Give yourself time. Time invested here will mean that when you really focus and go for it you'll be absolutely sure you're heading in the right direction.

Part 2

Do only what matters

Do only what matters

Now, obviously you can't literally only do the thing you identified as your purpose in that last chapter. But, you should be able to draw clear lines from everything you are doing to how they help you to move towards your vision of success. Whether that's taking time in your life to exercise or get outside into nature because you know that supporting your health underpins being able to do anything well, or it's spending time on the relationships which are your support network to help keep you on track when things go wrong. It's about being intentional about what you are choosing to spend your time and energy on. In this section particularly we'll take learnings from the work of the stoics of ancient Greece and the modern minimalists.

We'll also then look at how you create a focus in your work-life which enables you to metaphorically 'put the blinkers on' and be single-minded about the actions you need to take to move forwards with purpose.

It can be helpful to think of it as 'simplicity' helping us to understand what we should be doing, and 'focus' being how we make sure we do it and aren't distracted.

3 - Simplicity

Simplicity in life is about removing the unnecessary drains on our resources, emotions and time. We'll look in this chapter at different ways to identify the things which matter and those that don't, and how to eliminate the ones which don't.

Your work-life and your purpose

In the previous chapter you identified your purpose. It's important to understand how your work-life fits into that so that you can make decisions which help you to move in the right direction with pace and intention.

Your work-life may only contribute in terms of the money that you earn to give you the freedom to pay the bills and spend your time working on your purpose. In this case, it's about understanding how you can generate the money you need as effectively as possible and understanding exactly what your financial needs actually are. Then simplifying by removing those things you don't really need. It may mean you need less money to sustain you than you thought or can achieve your financial goals in less time, freeing you up to do what really matters.

Conversely, your work-life may be a fundamental part of your purpose and you may be looking to simplify outside of work to enable you to focus more on what you are doing through your job and deliver the greatest benefit you can.

The key here is to understand your own personal motivations and to not make any assumptions about yourself or others based on the specific job you have. For example, two nurses may have completely different purposes, one who's purpose is caring for people, the other who earns money nursing that to fund their mountaineering hobby which is their purpose. It's really important to remember that this doesn't mean that either of them are less good at their job or less committed to doing it well. But it does mean they need to understand and arrange their work lives to suit themselves whilst also doing a great job. Neither of these purposes are any less valid or worthwhile either. They are a reflection of what matters most to that individual at that time.

Having worked in the charity sector I have often heard people making assumptions about the motivations of others for working at an organisation and an expectation that everyone's work-life is also their purpose. Firstly, it's just not true. Secondly, it can mean that managers don't treat people as individuals and can have unfair expectations on people. And, thirdly, it implies a link between the level of passion for the mission of the organisation and performance, which also doesn't exist. There will be people at every organisation who are there to pay the bills but are also exceptionally high performers.

Simplifying your life

Although we are focusing on your work-life here, it's important to recognise that simplifying across your entire life can bring you significant benefits in terms of your wellbeing and enjoyment of your existence. I often think about it in three dimensions:

- Resources
- Time
- Energy

When it comes to resources, much of this is around our money and our material possessions. There are absolutely loads of ideas and resources around about this through the minimalist and decluttering movements.

Minimalism started in the 60s and 70s as a design aesthetic, however, over the last 50 years it has developed into much more of a lifestyle choice. The basic premise is that you should only keep in your life the minimum number of things you need to do what you want to do. There are lots of well-known names in this area: Marie Kondo, talks about it as only keeping those things that spark joy, whilst Stacey Soloman helps people clear the clutter from their home with the focus on creating spaces for families to be together, and The Minimalists talk about the impact of minimising their possessions on their overall happiness.

The overall idea is that every item you have in your home, and even your home itself takes: money to buy; time, money and energy to maintain; and can bring negative emotions which hold you back. The more stuff you have, the bigger space you need, so the more money you are paying to keep those things. It's also more effort and time to clean them, look after them and fix them. Chances are you're not actually using much of the stuff you have at all. We tend to just use the same small proportion of our things over and over.

So, it's a great place to start to simplify your possessions. You can find loads of ideas for how to go about this online. This isn't a decluttering book, but it is an important part of simplifying. And once you've done the work, make sure you've thought about how you are going to make sure you don't slip into the trap of refilling your life with more stuff you don't need.

Whilst resources do take up our time, so do lots of other activities we don't really want to be doing. Whether that's doing housework, going to social occasions or anything else in our whirlwind of busyness.

Busyness has become a badge of honour for so many people both in work and outside of it. I'm sure we've all been drawn into the busyness Olympics at one time or another. But actually, freeing up time in our lives for the things that really matter is incredibly freeing. Making a conscious choice to step away from the constant need to fill every moment with an activity and choosing not to feel lazy if you aren't busy. Rest and relaxation are vital to our health and wellbeing, and actually often we are able to do our best thinking when we have time to let our minds wander and work through the more challenging questions.

We can also find ourselves doing things we really don't want to with our time in order to please people we don't even really care that much about. I think we've all been to social occasions we didn't want to go to because we felt obliged to and then sat ignored in the corner because actually it wasn't that important to the person who invited us that we went either. We can assume that if we're invited, saying no is a bad thing or will upset or offend. But, think to the times you've invited someone to something, it's usually because you think they'll enjoy it rather than because you'd be in any way upset if they didn't fancy it. So, we need to get better at saying no – politely, but without needing to justify ourselves. And, we need to be better at allowing ourselves to stop.

Minimalism and reducing the demands on our time have come together in the Slow Living movement. Again, if you'd like to read more about this there are loads of books, blogs and articles on it on the web from lots of different perspectives.

The final element in terms of simplifying from my perspective is energy. It's about making sure you are spending your energy on the things that matter most. Going much further back than the minimalists to the stoics of Ancient Greece.

Musonius Rufus said:

"We must concern ourselves absolutely with the things that are under our control and entrust the things not in our control to the universe."

For me, that's it in a nutshell. If you don't have the power to change something, don't waste your energy trying.

There is nothing more likely to drain your energy than fighting against something you have no ability to influence or change. It is exhausting and soul-destroying.

I like to think of our energy as we would our phone battery. You need to charge it regularly and for long enough. So, make sure you are giving yourself enough time for sleep. We can't make ourselves need less sleep, so don't fight it, plan for it. We also have some activities which drain more of our energy than others – actually physical activity is often less draining than spending emotional energy. So, think about the balance of things you are doing in your day – do you think your battery will last all day? Do you need to plan in some rest time or time in nature to recharge during the day? Think about the relationships you have in your life. Do you have some which drain you? Really think about whether maintaining those relationships is helping you to do what is most important to you.

When you have a good balance of energy usage, you should end your days tired but satisfied and ready for sleep, but not so exhausted you're running on empty or so stressed you aren't able to switch off an get the quality sleep you need.

You wouldn't expect your phone to keep working if you don't charge it and you know it won't last long if you don't charge it fully. So why do you expect that of yourself? Likewise, our phones have a longer life if we drain them fully and recharge them fully, so make sure the energy you do have is being funnelled into something of value and you might find you live longer!

Arranging your work to suit your life

One of the few good things which came out of living through the Covid pandemic was the complete change in attitudes towards flexible working. Previously homeworking, part-time working or flexible hours were widely considered to not be open to everyone and needing close monitoring as they were an excuse for slacking. Obviously, for anyone working this way it wasn't the case and this perception was really damaging. I worked one day from home for a couple of years before the pandemic and people used to apologise to me for calling me on my day off! It infuriated me because I was working as hard, if not harder, at home than I would have been in the office. However, thankfully those days are behind us and, whilst at the time of writing this book we are still working out what the right balance of time together and time at home is, we are moving much further forward in terms of measuring people by their outputs rather than the hours they are sat at their desk.

What this means is that in some industries, definitely not all, there is more flexibility in terms of hours and locations. For others, very little has changed. And a third group have seen a need to react to the changes in other people's working practices. For example, in the cafe industry there is an expectation of providing free, good quality Wi-Fi and a regular supply of coffee through the day as people work from what were leisure locations.

So, all these changes give us more flexibility about how we manage our work within our lives. Part of simplifying might be removing time spent commuting and being able to allocate that elsewhere to other activities which bring more value. For others it might be about replicating their commute when working from home through a walk either end of the day to help provide that separation between home and work.

By understanding the role of your work in your purpose you can then start to use that to shape its part in your days.

Activity 1 – Mapping your activities into your purpose

List out all of the main activities which take your resources, energy and time. It doesn't need to be granular, you could group into broad categories, eg. Sleep, Travel, Work, Exercise, etc. Think back over the last week and add them in. You have 168 hours in a week. Add the hours spent on this activity to your list for each thing.

Sleep – 56 hours
Exercise – 3 hours
Travel – 4 hours
Work – 37.5 hours
Housework –
Hobbies –
Etc.
TOTAL = 168 hours

It should add up to 168 – if you have a gap, create a new category for 'Miscellaneous'. This is likely to include when you've lost an hour of your life to scrolling instagram or Wikipedia rabbit holes. This is a no judgement exercise. It's just to be honest about where your time and energy is spent. Now for each of those items, give them a score:

0 – this activity doesn't help me towards my purpose at all. These are the things which are time, energy and resource drains. Maybe it's the long conversation you had with someone you don't even like because you felt obliged to be polite. Maybe it was scrolling through Instagram and making yourself feel bad for not matching up to the false perfection of other people's lives.

1 – this activity is an enabler for me to help me achieve my purpose. An enabler is something which doesn't directly move you towards your purpose, but you need it to get there. For example, sleep is essential for giving you energy and health but doesn't directly move you forward. Bringing in money is similar, for most people you need to put a roof over your head and food on the table so it's an enabler.

2 – this activity directly moves me forward in achieving my purpose. This could be planning your next trip, spending time with your family, volunteering at a cause which matters to you or anything else which is directly moving you towards your individual purpose.

Have a look at how your week shapes up by multiplying the number of hours in each type of activity by the score for that activity. For example, if you sleep for 8 hours you would multiply 8 by 1. The give yourself a total by adding each overall score together.

Score less than 160 – you should revisit whether you are spending too much of your time on things which aren't helping you at all. Also think about whether you are taking care of yourself enough.

Score 160-168 – you are likely to be either in a good place but not moving forward, or moving forward at the expense of looking after yourself.

Score more than 168 – chances are you have a good balance of enablers and activities which are helping you move forward, with minimal time spent on things which do neither. There is a risk here you are moving forward with your purpose and not spending time on your enablers. Make sure you are mindful of burnout.

How much of your time is actually moving you forwards? Are your enablers proportionate to what you need or are you building an unnecessary surplus?

Your work-life could be an enabler, or it could be a direct contributor to your purpose. Rarely is work neither. It may also have elements which are both.

Think about whether there are any actions you could take to get the balance right for you.

For example, if work is simply an enabler to bring in money but it's taking up the vast majority of your time (including travelling to an office every day) look at whether you are able to make changes to your work pattern which reduce this impact. Could you work from home to save the travel time and cost one day a week? Could you look at condensed hours to make your work work for you? If you are earning more money than you need to move forward with your purpose, could you reduce your hours or do a different job which is less draining on your energy, time or resources?

Try implementing one small change to give you the time, energy and resources to focus on your purpose. Do it consistently for a month. What impact does it have? You don't need to overhaul your whole life on one swift move (although you might do that if it feels right to you) but you can start to build new habits and changes in your life to simplify down to doing the things which will most help you move forward.

And, just to be clear, having fun and relaxing are absolutely enablers and may be direct contributors! This isn't about time boxing every 5 minutes of your life to a state of constant busyness. Time to rest, relax and let your mind wander is time well spent in a lot of cases.

Simplifying at work

So, if that's how to simplify your life overall, you can apply the same thinking to your work-life in terms of simplifying where you spend your resources, time and energy.

Your work-life resources are less about money and more about your skills and experiences. Where are you going to spend those to give you the greatest positive impact?

None of what I'm going to propose is groundbreaking or new. But, it is a reminder of the tools and approaches you can use to make sure you're spending your valuable time, resources and energy in the right places.

Setting your objectives

Let's start with objectives. Most organisations set objectives for employees on an annual basis. For many this is a bit of a tick box exercise. But actually, it's a really fantastic opportunity to make sure you are absolutely clear on what the expectations are on you and what the most important things are for you to be doing.

I usually suggest setting 5-6 objectives. Each one should be clearly aligned to the strategic objective of the organisation. Each one should focus on a specific area and have a specific measure of success which is directly related. For example, if one of your objectives is to grow your client base, it's really important to be clear on what counts as a new client, what level of growth would achieving this objective mean and when that would be measured. SMART objectives may or may not be new to you, but as a framework they are really helpful. A SMART objective is Specific, Measurable, Achievable, Relevant and Timed. So, in this case your objective might be:

To increase the number of clients who have purchased a service in the last 12 months from 75 in December 23 to 90 in December 24. This will contribute to achieving the organisation's strategic growth objective.

Your objectives should be focused on the outcomes you are looking to achieve, rather than the things you are going to do. They should also be things which are completely within your control. For example, if you have a project delivery goal to deliver within a particular timeframe but you aren't the decision maker, your ability to achieve that objective is in someone else's hands. You might instead choose to look at what you can do to enable the decisions makers, for example the production of accurate reporting and forecasting to enable good decision making.

If you have existing objectives, have a look at them and see if they are fit-for-purpose. If not, take some time to update them and discuss with your line manager. If you are self-employed or don't have a line manager, you can still take advantage of the value in having clear objectives and an annual objective setting process.

The Eisenhower Matrix

This is one option for prioritising your work. It looks at the importance of your work and the urgency to help you know what you should be focusing on.

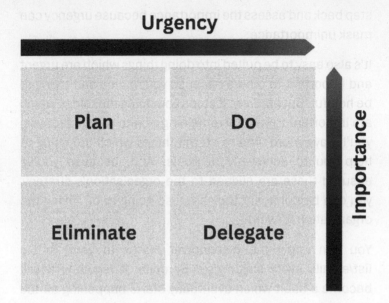

For every task assess its importance against your objectives. Those things that don't move you towards achieving any of your objectives are not important. Either delegate them to someone who they are important to or delete them from your To Do list.

Look at everything left on your list and note when it needs to be done by. If it's urgent and important, prioritise getting it done first. Then, work on the things which are important but not urgent.

When you look at what you have been working on, unless you are really good at doing this type of prioritisation you'll probably see that you've been drawn into dealing with lots of things in the urgent but not important space. When there are constant urgent asks coming in, it can be difficult to step back and assess the importance because urgency can mask unimportance.

It's also easy to be pulled into doing things which are urgent and important to others because you're nice and trying to be helpful. But actually, it stops you doing the things which are important to you. By remaining true to your objectives, you'll have more time to do the things which are going to help you to achieve your goals. And, because you've ensured these are aligned to the organisation's strategy, you can be confident they are also going to be taking the organisation forward.

You can apply the Eisenhower Matrix to your To Do list/emails every single day. By doing it regularly it will become a habit which eventually starts happening all the time without you having to consciously do it.

The Impact-Effort Matrix

The Eisenhower matrix is a great way of sorting through your task list. But, sometimes you need to decide which important things you are going to add to it in the first place.

Another great matrix to think about is the impact/effort matrix. Particularly if your work has parts which are direct contributors to your purpose and parts which aren't, you might want to consider that as your measure of impact. Otherwise, just think about the size of the impact towards achieving your objectives.

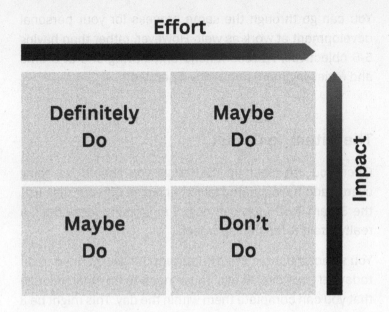

In line with our plan to simplify, the first thing to do is make sure you're not doing anything which is high effort, low reward. It's just not worth it. Likewise, make sure you are definitely doing the things which have a disproportionately high impact for the effort. The others are much more subjective. Things which have low effort, low reward can be good for filling gaps between the high effort work. High effort, high impact work is often where you can make the biggest strides forward, but you want a relatively small number of these.

These two matrices are my favourite simple ways to identify the things you should be removing from your work-life to simplify it down the activities which really matter.

You can go through the same process for your personal development at work as well. However, rather than having 5-6 objectives, I'd recommend only having one at a time and reviewing more frequently if needed.'

The 3 item To Do list

Once you are clear on the things you should be doing overall and have cleared everything else off your task list, the 3 item To Do list can help you simplify further. It's a really straight-forward approach.

You select the three most important things you need to do today off your overall list. These need to be small enough that you can complete them within the day. This might be 3 emails you need to respond to, one task as part of a bigger project or an important and urgent ask which is due today, and it is likely to be a combination of things. Work on these three things one at a time until they are complete. If you finish them all and have time remaining, go through the process again and choose the next three things. This approach can help to remove some of the mental clutter and noise which having a huge list to work through can cause. By simplifying down to just three tasks you have clarity over where you need to focus and a sense of achievement when you complete them.

Simplifying is core to enabling you to focus. The clearer you are on what you really need to be doing, the more time, effort and resource you can put into the things that really matter to you.

4 - Focus

If simplicity is about removing those things which aren't adding value to your life, then focus is about being single-minded about the things which remain. If something is important, which everything left on your work-list should be if you've put the suggestions in the last chapter into practice, then it deserves your full attention.

Our lives are full of distraction. Our attention spans are reducing and the skill of focus is being eroded. Multi-tasking is held up as something to aspire towards and to be valued. But actually, our brains can only do one thing at a time. This means that multi-tasking is really constantly switching from one task to another. This is deeply inefficient.

Imagine you are sat on the sofa one evening with your partner. You plan on spending time together watching a programme on TV that you've been wanting to watch for ages. You've got your mobile with you and have a blog post you want to read (from enikma.co.uk of course!). While your partner finds the programme and gets set up, you start reading the blog, you don't get far through when the music starts for the programme and you look up, a couple of minutes in your phone pings and you get a message from your friend who is having some relationship issues and wants your advice. You type out a message, then flick to the blog and reread the last few sentences before reading on. You realise you've started looking at your phone not the TV and put it down to start watching. Your partner asks you what you think of what's happening but you can't really engage with the conversation because you're not sure and trying to concentrate on the programme to catch up. This cycle continues all throughout the programme.

What's the outcome of trying to multitask?

1. You've reread the same bits of the blog post 15 times, still haven't finished it and really need to start again.

2. Your friend has only had a few messages when actually a proper conversation was what they needed.

3. Your partner feels that you haven't engaged with them because you were distracted by your phone.

4. You haven't enjoyed the programme, don't know what's going on and feel you need to watch it again.

By practicing focus, you could have watched the programme and left your phone in another room. You wouldn't have been distracted by pings or blogs. You could have agreed with your partner that you are going to talk about it after it's finished or paused for discussions during the ad breaks. You could have responded to your friend that you want to give them the time they need and planned in a time when you could speak to each other properly. You could have waited to start the programme until you'd finished reading your blog post.

This is happening to us all the time. Our systems and processes are set up to constantly alert us to new things and pull our attention away from what it is we are trying to do.

If something is worth doing, it's worth setting up a situation which allows you to be present and give it your full focused attention. You'll work faster, think more deeply and build better relationships.

One of the worst offenders for this are reminders and notifications. They work with our psychology to try to get us to behave in certain ways. That little red dot on your app, or the envelope telling you that you have mail is pretty irresistible to our brains. We want to know what it is and are immediately pulled out of our focus as soon as we see it, even if we don't actually do anything, just seeing it will have broken that focused attention. I'd really advocate for turning off notifications wherever possible. Alarms which help you manage your times/appointments are absolutely fine – their literal job is to break your focus so you don't miss other important and time sensitive things, but use them sparingly and where you really need them.

Focus in the modern workplace

Our modern, digitally-enabled workplaces have exacerbated this problem. We often feel that it is expected that we will be immediately responsive and our communication methods have multiplied massively in both speed and complexity. This can build the sense that everything is urgent. Many of us are dealing with emails, phone calls, instant chats, video calls, whatsapp messages and more all day long. Switching off to that is hard and requires conscious practice.

But, the value it brings is immense. For those of us working in an office setting, you'll inevitably have found yourself at some point in a meeting or conversation while also trying to respond to emails. Your brain can't possibly do both things at the same time, so chances are you're not really doing either properly. And is there anything worse than having to admit when you're asked your opinion on something that you weren't listening. There are also more difficult outcomes from being physically there in meetings but not being really present. If decisions are being made and you're in the room, it will be assumed that you agree with those decisions. If you are distracted by other things you could find yourself associated with decisions which you don't feel comfortable with or fundamentally disagree with. You are better to not attend than to only be there in body but not in mind. Be conscious of the impacts of loss of focus. If something is important enough to be on your list or in your calendar, it's important enough to be present for and give your full attention. Be mindful of the unintended consequences of not being focused.

You've been through making sure everything you are going to do is important through simplifying, so it's important that you give it your full attention.

Some things you could try to help with focus at work:

- Turn off the notifications on your communication tools and set aside specific times when you are going to read and respond. You'd be amazed to realise that people don't actually expect instant responses most of the time.

- Make use of any 'Do Not Disturb' functionality on your systems to stop you getting distracted.

- Sit somewhere without connectivity. This is one of my absolute favourites. I don't need any will power not to check messages or my phone, they just don't arrive.

- Leave your phone elsewhere, put it in your bag or a drawer where it's out of sight. You can find yourself picking it up and turning it on purely out of habit. If it's not there you break that habit.

- Don't have multiple screens on unless you actually need them. Two screens can be brilliant for some jobs, but if you are on a video call they are an invitation to not focus entirely on the call.

- Go old school with your notetaking in meetings, use a paper and pen rather than tapping away at a laptop. It feels less like a barrier and the other person/people can actually see that what you are writing is about the topic, so they feel more listened to and have evidence that you are engaged.

- Don't sit with your favourite group of chat buddies if you need to get something done. You can physically split yourself off if you love getting involved in a good gossip. Be honest and tell them you need to concentrate so they don't seek you out to distract themselves.

You will know your weaknesses when it comes to being distracted. Once you are clear on what these are, you can put in place changes which will help you to focus. Make one small change at a time and consciously do it consistently until it becomes unconscious. It takes time to build new habits and break old ones, but we're actually very good at learning new things and creating new pathways in our brains as long as we are consistent.

You are likely to feel a bit weird switching off from the things that usually distract you. You might even feel a bit anxious or jittery. That feeling will pass as your new way of working becomes normal. Likewise, others will adapt to your new ways of working and adjust their expectations accordingly. People who use tactics like emailing, then messaging to tell you they've sent an email, then calling to check you've received their message will soon find someone else to push their tasks on to if you stop responding immediately (or push back the tasks which you now realise aren't important). They won't think any worse of you, at the end of the day this kind of behaviour is just taking advantage of people's good natures. Once you've established your new ways of working, you'll likely spot unusual behaviours which you absolutely do need to respond to. Very few people pick up the phone to call, but if something really is important and urgent and you haven't responded in other ways, you can be sure the phone will start ringing. That's great and helps you to be able to identify the rare times when there really is an emergency. For example, I am absolutely happy to ignore any call to my mobile except if I see it's my kid's school phoning. I pick those up every time.

Creating a physical work environment

Whilst I've said this isn't a book about decluttering, I do think there is absolutely value in decluttering your physical and digital workspaces to enable you to reduce distractions and feel calm during your work time.

Piles of papers and digital clutter both make it more difficult to find the things you need exactly when you need them. Nothing breaks focus as quickly as having to hunt for the things you need to do the task. Not only that, the more you have around you, the more you have to draw your attention.

The ideal work environment is calm and uncluttered. You have space to set yourself up to work comfortably and you have the tools and information you need to do the job in a focused way. No matter what your work, you can set yourself up for success. For example, say you were a dance instructor teaching at a variety of venues. You might set up a station in your home with all of the items you need in set places. You have a list for each day of what equipment you need and lay it out in a specific way in your car so you aren't hunting for things and arriving stressed at classes. You might move all of the things your family need out of the car when you are using it for work. This helps you not to have to search through things that are not important for that activity and just focus on the one you are going into. You can then swap them back at family time. It can be a good mental break to divide between work and home to have a physical change to define the modes you are operating in.

The same applies if you are in an office job. Whilst there was a big push against hot-desking when it started to grow in popularity, actually it creates the environment for a simple and streamlined work environment. Not having your family pics on your desk doesn't make you love them any less, but it does save you time getting them out every day and carrying them to and from work. It also stops it from distracting you from what you need to be focusing on during the working day.

Having a simple and structured approach to the physical things you need to do your job can mean much less time organising and looking after items which aren't adding any value to your workday.

In exactly the same way, time spent organising your digital clutter is also key to making it easy to focus. Being able to quickly locate files you need enables you to retain your focus on the task. As soon as you need to hunt for something, you have to divert your attention away from what you are doing and use that brain power to find what you need. Much like multi-tasking, anything which stops your flow of work means time wasted trying to refocus on what you were doing and the loss of trains of thought. You can factor a digital clean up into your regular task lists. You'll know whether this will work for you best as a daily, weekly, monthly or annual task.

So, well worth spending some time setting your physical environment up to support your focus. It's setting yourself up for success and when you move into that physical work zone, you'll be creating triggers in your head that tell you that you are now switching into work mode. Delineation between work and home can be really helpful in reducing stress.

If you work from home and don't have a separate space, you can still apply the same principles by effectively creating a hot-desking arrangement by packing up your things at the end of the day. This makes the morning set up part of your ritual to get yourself ready for work. Alternatively, creating a screen or just covering over your workspace when you finish for the day can be really helpful.

Again, this is about what works for you. Try different approaches and see what fits. Consciously practice new habits to start building those mental triggers so they become normal.

Setting time boundaries

We will look at this more in the time and productivity sections, but it's important to recognise that as humans we do have a limited capacity for focused work. This is estimated to be a maximum of 3-4 hours of focused work per day. There are also lots of different ways to break that up depending on your own skills.

Some people, particularly those with ADHD (attention deficit hyperactivity disorder) or ASD (autistic spectrum disorder) can experience periods of hyperfocus. This is both a super-power and a challenge. It leads to long periods of deep focus on a particular task or thought linked to a lack of awareness of time or other things going on. Now if the focus is on something important then it can mean amazing results, but it's not something which can be turned on and off at will, so can also lead to long periods focusing on the wrong thing. Setting alarms and time boundaries as a matter of course can be helpful to force people to stop their periods of concentration and make a choice about whether to continue or move on to the next planned task.

Most of us find concentrating on one thing a real challenge, so if you've removed distractions, the next part is to think about how you are going to give yourself the right time periods of focused attention and the right breaks. Sometimes the breaks can be the moments when you find the answers.

For example, if you've set aside a couple of hours to do a data analysis task. You've been working at it for 45 minutes and you are starting to feel frustrated that you can't work out how to calculate on particular element. You decide to take a break and step away for a drink and a quick walk outside. During that walk you realise you are still thinking about the problem but just by letting your mind wander rather than it being in forced concentration. Suddenly you get the answer jump into your head from nowhere. I think we've all had times when this happens, whether it's straight away or a couple of days after walking away from a something which felt impossible to solve.

I can certainly relate to that during the writing of this book. Sometimes the words wouldn't flow. I knew what I wanted to say but couldn't quite get it to sound right or lost my way down a detail rabbit hole. When this happened I'd walk away from it for a couple of days. Almost everytime I picked it back up it was because the words came to me while I was lying in bed in the morning in the dark just letting my mind wander before starting the day.

Focus is absolutely essential for getting things done both well and quickly. But some tasks, particularly creative ones or those that require deep thinking can really benefit from planned breaks away doing something else. A good mix of activities can also help you feel a sense of accomplishment even if there's one activity which isn't quite there. Breaking these activities down can be really helpful so you are working towards the outcome rather than having a massive task on your list. You might even just want to set the tasks based on the time, for example, your 3 item To Do list might be:

- Send email to Dan

- Spend 1 hour working on (your big or difficult) project

- Speak to Claire about plan for next week

By time boxing that focused attention you'll need to give the project, you know you'll move it forward but rather than needing to get to a certain point, success is focusing on it for 1 hour. This approach can help to remove your inner critic that will be telling you that you can't do it if you don't reach a certain point in a fixed time. Stopping this negative internal dialogue means you're more likely to complete the overall project because you won't give up on it feeling like a failure.

So, in order to really enable yourself to focus and do your best work, start by setting yourself up for success.

1. Create an environment which minimises distractions for you.

2. Keep consciously practicing new focus habits, even when you slip, jump straight back to it.

3. Start small and see what works for you, then keep adding new elements. Wholesale change is hard to maintain.

4. Don't try to do everything, choose a few things to focus on which are most important, a never-ending To Do list can be overwhelming.

5. Set time boundaries to keep yourself on track. Both stopping hyperfocus taking over on the wrong

things and giving you a sense of accomplishment on the tougher things.

And be kind to yourself as you do these things, some days it will come easy, others will be really hard. Your new habits will take time to become unconscious for you. But, focusing on focus will enable you to do so much more, so much better. You'll build better relationships and feel more in control. And more than anything, you'll see yourself not just thinking or talking about what you want to do, but actually moving forward with your purpose

Part 3

Do more of what matters

Do more of what matters

As we move into the final section of the book, this is much more about the functional elements. How do we make sure our days are set up to enable us to achieve as much towards our purpose as possible? It's about giving ourselves the time and tools to build intentional momentum behind our work.

This brings together lots of shared wisdom on how to manage our time so we are able operate at our best. It's about understanding ourselves, our unique energy flows and using those to help us shape our days. It's also about giving ourselves the time we need to do the thinking and evaluating we need to remain focused.

We'll also look at productivity and how to get through as much as possible in a way that supports our mental health and enables us to take leaps rather than steps forward. This very much sits in the 'work smarter, rather than harder' space. We'll be reflecting back on your values to help you determine your own personal productivity approach which feels comfortable and authentically you.

5 - Time

"Time waits for no man"

Since the beginning of our existence as a human race time has continued to move forward. We have a finite amount of time on this earth and we don't know when it will run out for each of us. This chapter aims to help you get the most out of the time you have. As we talked about in simplicity, trying to change something you can't control is completely pointless and not good for anyone's mental health. Time we can't control. There's no point wishing we had more or regretting how we've spent our time so far. All we can do is take control of how we spend the time we have now.

Our society seems to have developed a narrative that you should be productive every second of every day. You should be getting up at the crack of dawn and have every 5 minutes of your day mapped out so you don't waste a single second of time. But, really, how enjoyable is that existence? Do you want to look back at the end of your life and see that you did a lot of stuff but were so busy doing it you never had time to enjoy it?

So, you've simplified and prioritised. You know what you want to do and you have systems, tools and the right environment to support you to focus on doing it. This section is much more about how you manage your time effectively to make sure you are moving forward with low stress levels and good health.

The basics for health

The first thing to think about is making sure you have enough time in your life for keeping yourself healthy. The key things are:

- Rest
- Movement
- Nourishment
- Nature

These are all things you need to factor into your life to support basic good health. Without good health it will be much more difficult for you to achieve your objectives and move forward with your purpose.

When it comes to rest, this is about making sure you are getting good quality sleep for enough hours each night.

There is absolutely loads of information and plenty of books out there on this subject, so definitely worth doing some wider research if sleep is a struggle for you.

Think about how much sleep you need. You will know what good sleep feels like to you. You may only need 7 hours a night or you might be more of a 9 hours kind of person. Listen to your body. Shortening your sleep time in order to try to give yourself more productive time is counter-productive. You will achieve much more in a shorter period if you are well rested.

As well as the actual time you are asleep, think about planning in your sleep preparation time. There is lots of evidence out there that being on screens just before bed is detrimental to good sleep. Try to factor in screen free time before you go to bed. There is also lots of evidence that building a regular sleep schedule is really helpful for promoting good rest. Going to bed and getting up at the same time everyday (even the weekends) is really helpful. I personally fought this for a long time, not wanting to believe that my weekend lie ins were unhelpful. However, I can honestly say that from personal experience this regular sleep pattern has been transformative in my energy levels and the quality of my sleep.

As well as good sleep, it's really important to keep our bodies moving. I have consciously said movement rather than exercise. We need to keep our bodies moving, but we don't need to always be giving it everything we have at the gym. Regular gentle exercise like walking, stretching and doing physical activities like housework or gardening are the minimum we need to do for health. Many of us have sedentary lifestyles, and our workdays can be especially so, and we need to consciously include regular movement throughout our days. We are not built to be still all the time. Think about how you are going to factor in movement in your day that works for you. Some of the below can be helpful ideas to try if you are struggling with how to fit it into your work-life:

- Switch a video call to a phone call and walk about while you are on the call.

- Try a standing desk to get out of a seated position for some or all of your day. Many workplaces will have these so worth working out where they are, or if you work from home you can get table top ones which sit on your existing desk.

- Try a walking meeting. These can be particularly good for one-to-one meetings with your team members or line manager. Interestingly walking side by side rather than looking directly at each other can be great for having more difficult conversations as it can feel less confrontational.

- Do some stretches between meetings. Even just rolling your neck and shoulders can help to release tensions that have built up.

- When you do have to get up (to get a drink or take a bathroom break) make it count by maybe going to the further away tea point or bathroom to get a few more steps in. You could throw some stretches in while you're at it.

The key is to focus on regular movement throughout the day wherever you can.

The next key area to consider is nutrition. Again, there is absolutely loads of information about different food and diet choices and it's not my area of expertise, so I'm not going to tell you what you should and shouldn't be eating. I would encourage you to think about it though and consciously choose things which will support your health and energy levels. I think we all know that surviving on coffee and junk food isn't going to give you the energy you need in the longer-term or set you up for a long, healthy and productive life. You'll know what the right options are for you.

The key is more about making sure that you make time for eating and drinking. Your brain will work better when its well hydrated and you'll struggle to concentrate if you are really hungry. On the other hand, you may find that you have a post lunch slump when your body is diverting its attentions from your brain to your digestive system, so think about how you manage which things you do when to take account of this.

The final element of basic health is nature. Now this one might seem a bit less obvious than the others, but time in nature has been shown to make a significant difference to mental health. Mental health is as important as physical health for a productive and happy life. And the two are not independent of each other. Access to nature doesn't mean having to walk in open countryside away from everything. Even in city centres you can find nature. When I'm in London for work, I often choose to walk rather than take the tube if I can and consciously look around me to find plants and animals. I look up at the sky and watch the clouds and I really enjoy finding where nature is fighting back. Weeds growing on pavements or out of walls, little sprouts of green in a grey landscape. You might have plants in the office or on the windowsill. Just notice them and be conscious of the nature all around you.

So, the first place to start is making sure that you have factored in enough time for these four key elements every day to maintain your health and overall wellbeing.

Know your energy flows

The next place to focus is on understanding your own personal energy flows both through the days, the months and the year. Each of us will have a unique flow of energy. For example, you might find your are at your most focused and productive in the evenings. If that's the case, following a prescribed time management process which assumes you are going to be super-focused first thing in the morning probably won't work for you. You might have one or more peaks during the day when you know you have the greatest capacity for focused work. Try to arrange your days to work with these. If you are an early bird who is able to easily focus in the early hours before the rest of the world is awake, plan your most focused activities for then. In this world of flexible working and varied work patterns, once you know your flow, you may be able to agree for a work pattern which best suits your needs. You have the power to break the expected 9-5 pattern if that works better for you.

You might also find that you have different productivity rhythms through the month. Particularly for women, the phase of your menstrual cycle can have significant impacts on your energy levels and the types of activities you are most suited to. Often women will find they are more creative and able to do big thinking tasks during the first half of their cycle, but are much more introspective and able to focus on more analytical or critical thinking activities during the second half of their cycle. This isn't a guarantee though. You will find your cycle impacts you in a unique way, but it can be helpful to map your preferences and what comes more easily over a few months to see your own patterns.

We also have annual patterns which impact on our energy levels. For example, in the northern hemisphere the Winters are long and the days short. The lack of sun leads to widespread Vitamin D deficiencies and the associated lack of energy. Understanding this can help you to organise when you focus on different things and to understand why you might want to dial back on activities in the Winter or allow for additional sleep time. The more you understand your own energy flows and cycles, the more you can plan your time to take advantage of them.

These cyclical patterns are often outside of your control. Whilst you can do things like Vitamin D supplements to help, try wherever possible to work with your energy flows rather than against them. There is no right or wrong and that's why a lot of the very prescriptive approaches to time management fail to deliver the promised results. It can be really disheartening to try to stick to someone else's timetable and see them having really amazing results but you not having the same outcome. Make sure you are setting yourself up for success by being uniquely you.

Setting boundaries

Once you know your own flow, you can start to be clear with others about what you need to do your best work. This may not work for their flow but you'll find the right compromise which works for you both if you are open and honest about it.

For example, if you know you are at your most focused between 8 and 10 in the morning, but your colleague is really chatty and distracted at this point in the day with their productive period being more in the afternoon, you need to come up with something that works.

You might decide to take yourself to sit somewhere different for that period of the day to give yourself time to get ahead with your own work. You can then rejoin knowing you've got the most important focus tasks done and can join in with the chat. Be honest with your colleague about it and maybe suggest that you have lunch together instead.

It's important that you also respect the needs of others when they are needing to focus. You'll find people who have a similar natural rhythm to you and can make sure you're giving everyone the opportunity to focus when it works for them.

That mutual agreement of what is social or more interactive time can be really helpful because you can both be really present for that time rather than frustrated that you wanted to be focusing. This will actually help your relationship as well because you'll be giving each other real attention. It can feel hard to have open conversations about this stuff, but actually, setting boundaries can be done in a really nice way and most people really value knowing what's going on. If people refuse to support you, you need to question their motives and why they are trying to sabotage your progress. As a two-way, respectful process, they should get benefits from it too. But managing change can be difficult, If you face resistance or hostility, it's worth looking into some of the tools and tips available for managing difficult conversations, giving feedback and managing change. There's a whole other book in that, so I won't cover it all here.

Energy givers and energy drainers

As well as our energy rhythms, different activities will either energise us or deplete our energy reserves. Much of this is linked to our personality type. For example, if you are an introvert you will likely find group activities and meetings energy draining, whilst individual work gives you energy. An extrovert will be the opposite. The same applies to whether you are a detail-oriented person or a big-picture person.

It's not about whether you are good or bad at the activity, it is much more about the type of activity or the method for doing it. You can be really good at something you find draining, and equally find things energising despite not being particularly good at them.

How you plan these different types of activities into your day can make a massive difference to how you are able to sustain your energy. Some things will be outside of your control, for example if you're invited to meetings you won't always be able to move them to suit your preferences, but you can make sure that you build the things you can control into your schedule to balance yourself.

Activity 1 – Map your energy levels

To understand how your energy levels are moving throughout the day, take a typical day and map out the activities you have in it.

For each activity note down the style of task – group, individual, meeting, etc.

Then the detail level of the thinking. Is it deeply detailed analytics at one extreme, high-level strategic concepts at the other, or somewhere in the middle?

Finally note the environment for the activity – will you be doing it at home, virtually or in a shared space?

Look at each of these elements and the tasks and identify whether they are an energy drainer or an energy giver to you.

Example

Task: Monthly budgeting
Type: Individual – energy drainer
Detail level: Detailed – energy drainer
Environment: Office – energy giver

As you can see, for this one task you may have a mixture of energy givers and energy drainers.

Do this for each activity through your day. What do you notice?

This exercise can often show why you find some days completely draining while others are very energising. If everything is coming together to drain you across all elements of most tasks, you can take steps to change things. For example, if you know you have some really draining tasks which you can't change the type or detail-level of, can you change the environment? You could also look at coming together in a group to all work on the same individual tasks so it changes the type.

It's about understanding what is within your control and what isn't. Then making choices about how you can make changes to those things in your control to make it work better for you.

It's also sometimes about changing the order of the tasks. When you are creating your 3 item To Do list, be mindful of the types of activities you are putting on there so you aren't inadvertently depleting your energy reserves.

Time blocking

Time blocking is a well-recognised tool for managing your time and ensuring you get everything done that you need to do. Much of the value in time blocking is that it removes the noise of a never-ending To Do list and no plan. You can relax and concentrate on the task in hand, knowing you have time to deal with the other tasks later. However, it can also be helpful to make sure you have a clear order of tasks which fits with both your energy flows and energy givers and drainers.

One of the things which can be really helpful in enabling focus is to also schedule time slots for looking at new messages and asks through the day. You can then easily respond or rejig your day if needed. You'll find you are still able to be very responsive to urgent work and changing priorities without it being overwhelming. I personally start work early, before most people are in. I begin by getting the most important thing I need to get done that day out of the way. I sit in the office because the background noise and people energise me, but away from risk of getting drawn into a day of chat. Once that's done I then review my messages and emails and make my time plan for the day. I check messages and emails again at lunch time and rejig my afternoon if needed. I check them a final time at the end of the day and create my 3 item To Do list for the next day. This is what works for me as a general pattern, but I definitely have days where it all goes off track! Your set up will need to work with your own flows and preferences.

Activity 2 – Time block a typical day

Look at the typical day you drew out earlier. Using that as a guide try time blocking it more effectively.

Start by blocking in the elements you can't control, eg. fixed meetings.

Look at what time you have around that and block in time for eating (and getting outside for some movement and nature if you can).

Now look at the time you have left. Break it down into chunks for each task you now need to complete. Think about the amount of time each task will take if you are doing only that task. Try to give enough time for completing the whole task in one slot if possible.

How does your day look? Do you need to move things around at all to balance your energy givers and drainers?

Think about what environment would best suit this day.

All of these things can help you to shape your days, weeks and months to support your purpose. They can be applied as much to your time outside of work as they are to your workdays. If your work is an enabler to your purpose, by using your time efficiently, you are more likely to find you aren't staying late or finding your outside of work time distracted by your in-work stress.

It's often a process of trial and error to get to a solution which works for you as an individual. No one else has the same energy flows and preferences as you, so make sure you are listening to yourself and how you work best. It would be much easier if I could just give you a timetable and guarantee it would work, but sadly that just isn't the way we are. If you can start to make time work for you, you will be amazed at what you can achieve with the same number of hours in the day.

6 - Productivity

So, now we have worked out how to make space in our schedules for doing all the things that matter. How do we make sure that that time moves us as far as possible towards our goal?

Everything you have already done to understand how to simplify and focus will already up your productivity massively, but there are some key things which can help you to get even more out of the time you have.

Busyness is not productivity

One of the key things I hope you take from reading this book is that busyness is absolutely not the same as productivity.

Busyness can stop productivity in its tracks, in fact, it's the very enemy of it.

'Busy' has become a standard response when asked how we are. It's worn like a badge of honour and I think we've all been drawn into the busyness Olympics at one stage or another. Often busyness is used as a proxy for importance, a myth which is reinforced by truisms such as 'if you want something done give it to someone busy'.

When you dig just a little deeper, you see that busyness is something which could be seen as a lack of control, organisation and prioritisation. It is often built on a constant response to the urgent, without much thought to the important. It's similar to people who work long hours all the time thinking it makes them look better at work. Actually, it can be seen as a lack of ability to manage time or achieve the job within the hours. If you are regularly having to work very long hours because you have an unrealistic workload, it's important to flag that to your line manager. Often managers are unaware unless you actively tell them.

High performers are generally those who aren't too busy to give themselves thinking time and focus on the important not urgent work. They are the people who leave work on time having done a great job and get a good balance between work and home which allows them to bring their relaxed, focused and ready selves to work.

But, it is so easy to get drawn into the busyness black hole and it takes conscious and intentional effort to climb out of it.

A first step can be to break the constant narrative of busy. Consciously make sure you don't use it as an answer to someone asking how you are. When they ask you, give them a positive response. If they respond with busy when you reciprocate, don't get drawn in. Just say 'I hope it improves soon'. Really subtly this starts to change the perception of busyness as a good thing. It's amazing how quickly you can change the perception of something by really simple changes. By implication, this response says busyness is a bad thing and also stops the conversation descending into a competition about whose life is busier.

Try it for a few weeks and see how you get on. Do people change how they start interacting with you?

If you are a line manager it's also really important to avoid the trap of giving those who are busiest the interesting and new work. To break the positive reinforcement of busy, it needs to be something seen as a blocker to getting opportunities. It starts to break down the trigger, action, reward cycle of habits by removing the reward.

So, apart from breaking the narrative around busyness, it's also important to understand the impact that reactiveness has on your ability to do the things that really matter. Productivity isn't just about getting a lot of things done, it should be about getting a lot of important things done.

I suggest a three-strand approach to building productivity:

- Specialise

- Delegate

- Automate

Together these can be powerful for a step-change in productivity.

Specialise

We've covered prioritisation in detail in the simplification chapter. It is absolutely core to making sure you are focusing on the right things. Another dimension which supports this is making sure that the right people are doing the right things. If something is really important but you don't really have the skills to do it, sometimes the best thing to do is to outsource it to someone who is a specialist. Trying to do everything yourself can be really inefficient as things you don't have the right skills for are going to take longer and likely not be done as well. The one place where this is worth persevering with is when this is a recognised development area for you and supports your current personal development objective. We all need to learn how to do things and improve our skills. But we don't need to be brilliant at everything all the time.

For example, if you are a business owner but you struggle with the regulations around tax. You are probably better off to pay an accountant to support you than to spend huge amounts of time and effort trying to do it yourself and risking getting it wrong. The time you save can be used doing what you are brilliant at, like bringing in new clients or delivering work.

The cheap option in terms of spend can often be a false economy as you could generate more income through focusing elsewhere. Spending your time in your strength and development areas are much more powerful in driving productivity than forcing yourself into your weakness areas.

Think about your own strength and weakness areas. Are you able to reduce or eliminate the work you are doing in your weakness areas to spend more time in your strength areas? Identify where you already have access to specialists and where you might have gaps you need to find people to fill.

Don't be afraid of using people for specific tasks, or things you think you should be able to do. We're all different and your weakness areas will be someone else's biggest strength. It can feel like you are keeping all the good stuff for yourself and giving the rubbish jobs to others, just remember, one person's trash is another person's treasure. We're not all the same and it's by recognising this that we can boost productivity.

Delegate

The next area to consider is delegation. You can delegate whether you are in a line management role or not. You can also delegate upwards.

As with specialisation, this is about making sure the right person is doing the right thing. The tasks you've mastered and now find boring might be exactly the development opportunity someone else is hoping to get. Likewise sometimes you need to delegate upwards if you work in a hierarchical organisation. You can fight the reality and try to change it and use your influence, or you can go the easy route and escalate. The right choice will depend on the exact situation. Sometimes you'll want to break the mould and sometimes you just need the result.

Delegation can be seen as a bit of a dirty word, assumed to mean shirking work and loading it onto others. But in reality, delegation is about getting the right people to do the right things, sharing the opportunities and working effectively within the culture, systems and processes of the organisation you work in. People who are great at delegation will build a reputation as someone who supports development and gets things done.

To delegate well you need to:

1. Understand the strengths and weaknesses of your team.

2. Understand the areas your team want to develop in.

3. Give people autonomy to do the tasks their own way and give them enough time to learn.

4. Be there to support and guide without dictating or taking over.

Only delegate tasks you know you can let go of. If you are going to micromanage the task or dictate exactly how it needs to be done, don't delegate it. It's disempowering to the person you are delegating to and ends up with two people doing it, rather than enabling you to do something else. This false delegation isn't helpful to anyone and can have the opposite impact on the people involved than great delegation.

Automate

Pretty much everyone will be using digital technologies in some way in their work lives. With that comes the power to automate tasks. My general rule is that anything repetitive, rules based and resource heavy should be automated.

Human brains are brilliant at reason and nuance. What they aren't that great at when compared to computers are monotony and accuracy. A human processing 25,000 of the same transactions through a process will almost certainly make mistakes, whether through tiredness, emotional changes or just losing concentration. A computer on the other hand will follow the process exactly the same each and every time, take the same time to complete it (likely less than the human) and provide completely consistent outputs that follow the rules set. We should be taking advantage of this. It's not different to specialising really. Computers are specialists at repetitive, rules-based processes and humans aren't. Let the computers do what they are best at and free us up for doing the things computers just can't do so well.

The key with automation is that the outputs are only as good as the inputs and the rules. The time spent in making sure that the automations are set up correctly will massively improve the overall impact of automation.

At a really basic level there are inbuilt automation tools in most email programmes that allow you to set rules on what to do with incoming mails. Perhaps you want to set up a rule which moves certain regular emails into a specific folder so you know where it is when you come to do your review. This is aligned with setting up your digital environment to make it easy to maintain focus by knowing where to find information.

You might also have automations in your calendar – whether that's repeating reminders and time slots to setting rules which make all your meetings start at 5 past the hour to give you a context switching, bathroom and drink break between each session. You are probably using more automations than you realise.

Look at the tools and systems you have. What options are there for simple automations which would save you time doing repetitive tasks? Set some time aside for understanding what you already have. You may never have noticed the options available to you.

Setting up automations might be an area where you want to work with a specialist. But, in many cases software providers have really intuitive easy to use tools which you can easily set up and manage yourself once you know they are there. With the rise in artificial intelligence enabled tools, it is becoming easier and easier to set up automations without any knowledge of how they work.

Time you invest in getting these systems set up can pay back really quickly in time saved. Some people have managed to set up businesses which almost entirely self-run through automation, allowing them to reap the rewards whilst spending their time doing other things. If you think this is for you, you might enjoy reading The 4 hour Workweek by Timothy Ferriss.

For most of us, automation is one part of a series of activities we undertake to boost our productivity.

Productivity with an intangible output

So you've freed up your time to do the things that matter. But how do you rationalise those activities which don't have a tangible output?

Productivity isn't all about doing as much as possible. It's also about doing the things which will enable us to do as much as possible. This is often the space where the intangible productivity activities sit. Going for a long walk and thinking about a problem or idea can feel not very productive. But, it's this time which enables us to produce at pace once we get started.

If you are someone who has a tendency to jump straight in, this can feel really hard. Reflectors will be really accustomed to taking a step back and considering their next step before jumping in. This can feel frustratingly slow to others. But, this time is really important in considering and evolving options. I'm sure we've all heard the phrase 'Failing to plan is planning to fail'. It applies to not giving yourself enough time to think things through, be creative and make sure you've considered all angles. You might do this on your own, with others or both.

The important thing to remember is that this is productive time. This is absolutely going to enable you to deliver more, quicker and better when you get into delivery mode. It will reduce rework and mean your activities have a higher chance of success. Reframing productivity so it's less about physical outputs and more about all of the elements of moving forward with intention and purpose can be a game changing switch in mindset.

This also applies in your life outside of work. Relaxation isn't not being productive. If your purpose is to have an enjoyable life, maybe time spend sipping that coffee in the garden or chilling with your friends of an evening is the most productive time of your day and taking you forward with your purpose more than any amount of work churn.

That down time might also be the enabler which balances your life and gives you the headspace and energy to deliver your purpose day by day in your workplace. As long as you are choosing what you do intentionally, then you are likely choosing things which are moving your forward. At its core, increasing productivity is simply being selective about what you do with your time and giving it your full focus. If you don't know where your time has gone – hello scrolling social media – then that is the signal you probably need to think about how you increase your productivity. Being intentional about where you spend your time, energy and resources and by default you will be being productive.

Conclusion

I said in the introduction to this book that The Enikma Philosophy was simple. And it is.

1. Know what matters
2. Do only what matters
3. Do more of what matters

But, as you've seen. Without intentional and conscious practice, it's so easy to slip back into old ways of thinking and behaving.

As humans, we are built to value and seek belonging, and with belonging come norms and conformity. So, stepping out of that and doing something a bit different takes courage and conviction. But it is only by doing this that you can be part of a movement which has the power to change how we all operate as a human race. Rather than following the norms and behaviours of the past, you can be a change maker, setting the norms of the future.

For me, I feel my purpose is to help others through sharing my learnings on how to develop an intentional career for a purposeful life. I didn't write this book thinking it would make me rich or famous! Money is a great enabler, but it won't bring me a life of contentment. So, I actively encourage you to pass this book on to someone you think would benefit from it and has the potential to join our movement rather than encouraging them to buy their own copy. It's better for the environment and it helps to create that feeling of belonging we all need. Why not write your name, the year and your what you're going to do differently on the last pages before you share it?

If you're reading an ebook or listening to an audio book, you can add your name to the 'Creating a Movement' page online at enikma.co.uk to take part.

So, what are you waiting for, go and do what matters!

Further reading

There are some really great books which have helped me shape this philosophy and might help to give you more depth to your understanding of certain areas. However, before diving in and reading these, a word of caution. I started this book by pointing out that there is a risk you spend so long reading about being intentional and productive, it actual stops you putting it into practice. Just be mindful and consider if you are at risk of doing that. Maybe try making some changes now and only reaching for some more reading once you've seen how it's gone.

Habits

Atomic Habits
by James Clear

The Power of Habit
by Charles Duhigg, Mike Chaimberlain et al.

The 7 Habits of Highly Effective People
by Stephen Covey

Automation

The 4 Hour Work Week
by Timothy Ferriss

Prioritisation

The 4 Disciplines of Execution
by Chris McChesney, Jim Huling, and Sean Covey

Activities

There are a number of activities throughout the book which you can use to help you shape your intentional career.

Values

Purpose

Acknowledgements

I am incredibly lucky to have been supported in developing this book by a fantastic group of people who have been active in helping me shape this approach, let me use them as guinea pigs and been there to support me when I've lost my way.

When you're writing a book on how to have an intentional and satisfying career, there's definitely a high pressure to practice what you preach. As I've said throughout, the process is simple, the application is a challenge. Just like everyone else, I have the same challenges in my own work-life and keep having to bring myself back to what matters.

So, for those who've been on this journey with me and there when I've needed it to nudge me forward. Simone, Kate,

Gemma, Leanne, Jaime, Vicky, Karen, Frankie, Isabelle and Rich. Thank you.

But mainly my thanks have to go to my family who are my cheerleaders and have had to endure me trying to get them to follow my advice for years. Stu for, well, everything. Jay for being the most positive supporter, knowing when I need a bit of validation and encouragement. Ryan for the hours of coffee, walking and talking, mutually helping each other be better when it's been hard. And Philippa for reminding me every day what is possible to achieve as a woman with focus and determination.

Creating a movement

Add your name, the year and your thoughts here before you share the book.